The

Mysterious
North Shore
of Lake Superior

The Mysterious North Shore
of Lake Superior

A Collection of Short Stories About
Ghosts, UFOs, Shipwrecks and More

by William Mayo & Kate Barthel

Adventure Publications, Inc.
Cambridge, Minnesota

ACKNOWLEDGMENTS

I would like to thank everyone who contributed their personal stories to be included here and all the many friends and acquaintances from the past and present who strongly encouraged the writing of this book. But mostly to my children, Melanie, Jessica, Kelsey, Kate, Brenna and Bill, who sustain my heart, give me courage and never let me forget what's important.

—Bill

Reading together. We passed time this way on the couch, in the car, tent and just about anywhere you can imagine. We thought about bigger ideas and talked about grander possibilities. Dad, my three brothers, my sister and I traveled through time and space led by Mom's fluid voice echoing the page. Then you and I filled all our spare minutes doing the same and now you are bringing the circle round again. Thank you, Johnny, my boy, for showing me the book that helped set the wheels in motion for this one.

—Kate

Edited by Ryan Jacobson and Dan Johnson
Cover illustration by Bill Mayo
Cover and book design by Jonathan Norberg

10 9 8 7 6 5 4 3 2

TABLE OF CONTENTS

Ghosts and Spirits

GHOSTLY SHIPMATES

O Captain! my Captain! our fearful trip is done;
The ship has weather'd every rack, the prize we sought is won;
The port is near, the bells I hear, the people all exulting,
While follow eyes the steady keel, the vessel grim and daring;
But O heart! heart! heart!
O the bleeding drops of red,
Where on the deck my Captain lies,
Fallen cold and dead.

—Walt Whitman, Leaves of Grass

Ore boats have long histories. They plow up and down Lake Superior, many of them painted in the same rusty hue as the cargo they carry. They seem unremarkable, especially in the port cities where they come and go with regularity. Many of them, though, could tell stories of storms and struggles worthy of books—if only they could speak.

The *American Victory* is one such boat. It's a fitting name for the old ore freighter, though she's been called many others. In 1943, she entered military service as the *Neshanic*. Serving as an oiler, she participated in nearly every major battle in the South Pacific as Allied forces fought their way toward Tokyo. She served her country with honor, was decommissioned in 1945 and received nine battle stars.

In 1947, she was purchased by the Gulf Oil company and renamed the *S.S. Gulfoil*. She worked hard without mishap for more than ten years, but then disaster struck in August of 1958.

Sailing empty and outbound from Providence, Rhode Island, on her way to Port Arthur in Texas, the *Gulfoil* found herself near the mouth of Narragansett Bay, enveloped by a thick fog. Running blind, yet cruising nearly at full speed, the freighter was taken off guard by the sudden appearance of the *M.V.S.E. Graham*, fully loaded and carrying six hundred thousand gallons of fuel.

The crew aboard the *Gulfoil* spotted the *Graham* too late.

Unable to steer clear of the *Graham*, the *Gulfoil* rammed her bow into the tanker, gashing a huge hole in her side. Gasoline poured from the *Graham's* wound, while sparks from the collision ignited the explosive cargo. Within seconds, both vessels were wrapped in fire.

Harbor tugs, naval firefighting units and Coast Guard vessels worked all day, through the night and into the following day to bring the fire under control. By the time the blaze was extinguished and the smoke cleared, the *Gulfoil* had lost seventeen souls out of a compliment of thirty-eight. The *Graham* didn't lose a man, her crew having jumped ship moments after the impact.

The remains of the *Gulfoil's* captain, Eden Montrivell, were discovered on the ship's bridge—indicating that he never left his post. Eight more bodies were recovered in the crew's quarters, another eight were found floating in the sea. The bodies were all removed, though some of the *Gulfoil's* crew are said to still inhabit her today.

After Marine Board investigators found both ships at fault—the *Graham* for not posting a proper lookout and the *Gulfoil* for faulty navigation and excessive speed—the *Gulfoil* was moved to the Maryland Shipbuilding and Dry Dock company in Baltimore, Maryland, where she remained until 1960. It was then that the nearly gutted hull was picked up by the Pioneer Steamship Company, rebuilt as a Great Lakes bulk carrier and renamed the *Pioneer Challenger*.

A run-in with a submerged rock in Lake Erie cut her tenure with Pioneer Steamship Company short, but her next boss was Oglebay Norton Company, who named her the *Middletown*. It was during her forty-four years of hauling taconite pellets, from the iron ports of the north to the steel mills on the lower lakes, that stories of the paranormal began to surface.

I had the chance to interview a former *Middletown* crewman named Steve, who experienced several ghostly encounters firsthand. Any seaman will tell you that ship doors are tightly closed. Latches are checked and double-checked, especially in the potentially deadly seas of Lake Superior. So when doors began to mysteriously swing open, Steve knew that something was amiss. Unseen hands seemed to be at work. Perhaps the old crew and the new crew were crossing paths.

Over his remaining days and months aboard the *Middletown*, Steve's encounters with the supernatural seemed to escalate. Strange, unnatural occurrences grew in frequency until one night he was awakened from a deep sleep. He was used to awakening in the middle of the night to a pitch-black cabin, but on this night he was able to make out the figure of a man looming over his bunk. The frightful sight snapped him to alertness, which was when he realized the figure was oddly luminescent. Unable to comprehend what he was seeing, Steve stared for a long moment at the glowing phantom, and slowly began to grasp that this was no living man. In that moment, the ghost melted away.

To this day, word around the ports of Lake Superior is that this boat carries more crew than is accounted for on the payroll. Yet despite these reports, the boat was sold in 2006 for nearly $120 million. She remains one of the fastest ore boats on the Great Lakes, and as she nears the end of a long career, she finally has a name reflecting her dignity: *American Victory*. Should you happen to see her on a trip across Lake Superior, look for the proud symbol of her earliest career—the yellow World War II ribbons on her bridge wings. Wish her safe passage and remember those who lost their lives aboard her, those who visit her still in the night's shadows, loathe to relinquish their orders for a ship "grim and daring."

SPACE BETWEEN: RITA'S STORY

Somewhere over the rainbow
Bluebirds fly.
Birds fly over the rainbow.
Why then, oh why can't I?

—E.Y. Harburg, Over The Rainbow

Whatever you believe about the nature of miracles, we ask that you consider this story: a story that is true, a story of home and of wishes granted—a story of sleep and dreams, of love and longing. Rita's story.

We stopped by Roy's farm one morning. Roy was a longtime neighbor of Bill. We had heard the news of his wife's death and wanted to check in on him. The first thing Roy said to me was, "Sorry things are in such a state. I've had a hard time since my wife passed away." Consumed with his grief, he put it out there in the open. Though we tend to painfully avoid the topic, it is a paradox that won't ever go away for any of us. It is so incomprehensible, how do you talk about it—yet so vast, how do you not talk about it?

We chatted about the wildlife he had seen lately from the kitchen window, his horses and his bad knee. Through it all, he reminded us that his wife was missing, and remembered things she'd said or done—especially her fondness of animals. Sad and struggling to make conversation, he stared at the stacks of paper on the table. Then he looked at us sharply and said, "I have something to show you," and abruptly left the room.

He returned with framed pictures. One look at the astonishing photographs left us no doubt that something amazing had happened, and the mystery of it took us utterly off guard. The pictures told a story about the space between worlds—where anything is possible.

We were eager to hear more about these strange photos, and Roy wanted to talk about Rita, filling the void of her absence with memories. Somehow by telling them, he created a measure of comfort for himself. More than that, in his struggle to understand the enormous puzzle of what happens to us after life, he clearly yearned to give this remarkable woman just homage. How they had lived and cared for each other was an integral part of what he had to convey; he almost felt obligated to share with us.

Roy and Rita met when they were growing up in Deerwood, Minnesota. They eventually settled in Two Harbors with a farm of their own. It was 1962 and despite the local opinion that they paid way too much for the place, they knew that they had found somewhere to make home. Priceless. They worked hard to make the life they wanted.

In the space between day and night, when the sun had set and the day sounds were yielding to silence, they found time on summer evenings to reconnect with each other, and enjoy what simple pleasures they were both so fond of in nature. Before darkness fell or the night sounds arrived, they would set aside their many tasks of barn and house and sit on the porch to listen to the quiet. Knowing that this was the best part of the day, they would hold hands and be still together.

By all accounts, Rita was one of the warmest, most spiritual people you could ever hope to meet. This made the news of her cancer even more difficult for her loved ones. By the summer of 2005, it was apparent to everyone that Rita was dying. She and Roy had been through difficult times, but the last few years had found them growing even closer. In Roy's own words, "We never wanted to be away from each other, like teenagers." True to form, Rita was more concerned about her husband being on his own than with her own illness.

Rita became weaker and eventually spent all of her time on the living room couch. Family and friends passed through to visit. With each new day her slumber grew deeper and lasted longer. Finally, by August 27, Rita did not awaken, and spent the rest of her time on this earth wrapped in sleep.

At the same time, in her childhood home of Deerwood, strange events were unfolding. Back at the farm where Rita had grown up, the current owner, Laurie, left to pick up her grandson. When she arrived at her daughter's house a quarter mile away, she noticed a female marsh hawk perched on the roof. From inside the house, she watched as it came near a large window and appeared to be keenly observing her grandson playing on the other side of the glass. Curious, Laurie approached the bird, expecting it to fly away as the door opened, but it did not.

Strangely overcome with a desire to connect with the hawk, Laurie drew nearer. As if in a dream and feeling a little enchanted, she found herself offering her arm to it, using only her thin sweatshirt as protection from its sharp claws. She could scarcely believe what was happening when the hawk accepted the perch. It gently rested there, its hooked beak just inches from her face. The hawk gazed at her, looking intently into her eyes with an air of calm regard. Interested, but not sure what to make of this wild creature's lack of fear, she and her grandson left for home.

Laurie couldn't imagine her day getting any more bizarre, but when she pulled into her farm, the marsh hawk was waiting for her.

Perched on the peak of her barn, it was the identical size and bore the same markings as the one just seen at her daughter's. It had to be the same one. Intrigued, Laurie spoke to the bird and it flew to a branch near her, then to the ground at her feet. She could see that it was not injured and appeared to be quite healthy, evidenced by the bright gleam in its eyes. Laurie felt an odd sense that the bird not only lacked apprehension about being near her, but that there was some familiarity in the way it looked at her.

For the next hour and a half, Laurie and the bird continued their interactions. Wherever she went, the bird followed. Incredibly, at one point it even walked onto her grandson's lap as he sat on the ground. Laurie grabbed her camera and snapped several photographs of the hawk.

Feeling overwhelmed and mystified, Laurie went into the house to call her sister. She sensed strongly that there was some task at hand that she was being called to do; the hawk was trying to tell her something.

As coincidence would have it (or perhaps it wasn't coincidence at all) Laurie's sister Amy lived in Two Harbors, just down the road from Roy and Rita. As Laurie blurted out her story, Amy listened in stunned silence.

"What does it mean?" asked Laurie.

Amy responded, "It's Rita."

In a state of awe and clarity, Laurie went back out to the hawk. As they gazed directly at each other, Laurie asked, "Are you Rita?" As the words fell from her lips, the hawk snapped out of its calm demeanor. Its wildness returned. It crouched down and then took flight, retreating to the peak of the house, lighting for a moment directly above the window of Rita's childhood bedroom. Then it wheeled into the evening. One last photograph caught the bird moving past Rita's bedroom in the fading light, its wings a blur of motion.

The next day, Rita's long and courageous battle with cancer ended. Yet in her passing—as in her life—she found a way to touch people's lives. This strange and mystical visitation by the female marsh hawk to Rita's childhood home, a place she surely held in a treasured part of her heart, came on a day she lay nearing death. Quite possibly, she was slipping back into old memories from her life, drifting back and forth between worlds.

Those who've heard the story have found it profoundly moving, and somehow very fitting for a woman who loved God's creatures as Rita did. She loved little children and little birds so much, she would make Roy leave patches of their much-needed hayfield undisturbed for mother birds with chicks. It is fitting that she may have found a way to fly back to her old home for a time, her spirit lifted by the wings of a powerful hawk, made gentle by Rita's kindly presence. Perhaps in recognition for her kindnesses, she was granted a wish, a moment to fly home once more. Wouldn't most of us do the same, given the chance? Maybe such things are sometimes allowed, in acknowledgement of a tender heart and sweet spirit. We like to think so.

THE DUTY OF GHOSTS

If you could read my mind, love,
What a tale my thoughts could tell.
Just like an old time movie,
About a ghost from a wishing well.
In a castle dark or a fortress strong,
With chains upon my feet,
You know that ghost is me.

—*Gordon Lightfoot*, If You Could Read My Mind

Split Rock Lighthouse State Park is perhaps the most frequently visited and most beloved historical site on the North Shore of Lake Superior. Yet its lighthouse operators (commonly known as keepers) and their assistants remain the unsung heroes of the sea. These men needed an unceasing dedication to duty, and the grit to keep the light burning—always, no matter the conditions or situation. Like a ship's captain who bears ultimate responsibility for the safety of his vessel and crew, the keeper also shares this burden, as all captains look to him for light and guidance.

The lighthouse and its accompanying fog signal building began operating in 1910. They were built in response to a brutal November gale in 1905 that is reported to have damaged twenty-nine vessels—seven of which were wrecked within twelve miles of the Split Rock River.

For the next 59 years, Split Rock's keepers warned nearby ships of the treacherous shoreline and impending doom. First powered by an incandescent kerosene lamp, and later by a one thousand-watt electric bulb, the light was said to have a range of twenty-two miles. The eerie fog signal could penetrate five miles of gloom.

Sadly, calamity struck within the lighthouse's first year of operation. Two of the head keeper's young assistants, whose duties included rowing to Beaver Bay to pick up mail and supplies, tragically drowned when their boat capsized. Apparently, despite the keeper's warnings, the duo had attached a makeshift sail to their boat. Because the small craft lacked a keel and was not designed for sailing, this risky rigging made it dangerously unstable.

When the young men failed to reach Beaver Bay, several locals ventured onto the big lake and found the forlorn little supply boat floating upside down—a sail secured to one of its seats. The assistants' bodies were never recovered, and their story seemed to be over almost before it began. But in a place such as the North Shore, where the paranormal seems a common thread in the very fabric of life, this was not the case.

Though Split Rock was decommissioned in 1969, it lives on today. Each year, tens of thousands of people visit the historic site and adjoining state park. Included in this throng are groups of wide-eyed schoolchildren, who arrive by the bus loads for special tours. Their visits commonly consist of walking the grounds, exploring the adjacent state park, an interpretive tour leading down to the lakeshore and the much-anticipated lighting of the lamp—a striking sight to behold. It was an airtight routine for a tour guide whom we'll call "Jon." At least, it was until the summer of 1990.

Through the gathering darkness of evening, Jon was leading a gaggle of excited children down to the water's edge. As he glanced behind him, he noticed in the distance a small light bobbing its way up the path, back toward the area from which Jon and his group had come. He had not met anyone on his way down, and he was not expecting any other staff members. Needless to say, Jon was puzzled.

Moments later, Jon heard something that chilled him to the core. Several children who had joined his group from an earlier tour were discussing a strange encounter they had experienced. The youngsters reported to Jon that they had seen a light coming across the lake, directly toward the beach. As curious children might, they had gone to investigate.

It wasn't long before they found what they were looking for. The light was coming from a small boat that had docked. Two strangely clad men disembarked—one holding an antiquated lantern, the other a bag. It appeared that some sort of reenactment was taking place, since both men were wearing old-fashioned work clothes. The children watched silently as the men quietly disappeared up the path, toward the top of the hill.

Jon was at a loss. He knew of no special, staged events that night. And after checking with other employees, he could find no explanation for what the children had seen.

It has been said that children can often see the mystical when adults cannot, for they are not yet blinded by dogma and cynicism. Did the young light tenders finally make it back to their post that night? It has been written that every lighthouse the world over has at least one ghost. Perhaps by its solitary nature, the work can only be understood by those who have done it. And these few must return from time to time, to revisit the world where they dreamed their dreams, communed with eternity and learned to become—over their long years of service—navigators of time.

SPLIT ROCK KEEPERS

. . . Many a man has served me,
Tending the Light with care,
Many a vanished footstep
Passed by my winding stair.
Years pass and men pass with them,
Never my light grows dim,
One hands the torch to another,
Others will follow him.
So are the centuries moving,
Still serving men am I,
Constant through gales of winter
Calm beneath summers sky.
Lights are the hope of seamen,
Warning of rock and shoal,
We are the danger-stations,
We are the sea-patrol!

—Hattie Vose Hall

Are ghosts real? If so, why do they exist? Is a ghost the shadow of a person who has passed from this earth? Is he somehow drawn back to the place that held him in life? Perhaps a ghost is a dream-walking spirit, returning once more to a world he could never forget. No living person can say for certain, which in part is why ghosts fascinate us so.

In August of 1997, Matt Miller and a younger co-worker, Zack, were wrapping up a typical day at Split Rock Lighthouse outside Two Harbors. They closed and locked up the place, then they started toward their vehicles. As they walked away from the grounds, a movement at the top of the lighthouse suddenly caught Zack's eye. He turned to Matt and asked, "Did you see that?"

Matt glanced back, and he too saw a dark figure moving beyond the lighthouse's glass windows. Almost certain that the lighthouse had been empty when they left it, the two men assumed they had mistakenly left its door unlocked.

They returned to the lighthouse, but the door was securely locked. Obviously, Matt and Zack had inadvertently locked someone inside. They gave the place a thorough inspection, but there was no one to be found.

In his fourteen years at the Split Rock Lighthouse Historical Site, Matt Miller heard several stories about guests encountering ghosts. In most cases, the guests mistook the spirits for employees dressed in time-period costumes. One of Matt's favorite tales involved a careless visitor who had lost his wallet.

It was the end of a hot, July day when the man returned to the lighthouse. He was disappointed to find its door closed and locked. Hoping that an employee or two might still be inside, the man knocked loudly on the door. When there was no answer, the desperate man persisted—this time knocking and shouting for someone to open up.

"Hello, is anyone in there?" yelled the man. "I think I left my wallet inside!"

He was about to give up when suddenly the door was flung open. A man mature in years, dressed in an antique keeper's uniform, unceremoniously pitched the wallet at the tourist and slammed the door shut. Of course, there are no such employees at the lighthouse.

Matt Miller has never been inclined to believe in the paranormal. After all, lighthouses naturally inspire thoughts of the romantic past, and people can be prone to flights of fancy. Still, he never did figure out what Zack and he saw on that August night. If it were a ghost, it's the first and only time he ever saw one—which is why it's an experience he will never forget.

THE TALL MAN

There are more things in Heaven and Earth, Horatio, than are dreamt of in your philosophy.

—*William Shakespeare,* Hamlet

A legend has arisen out of Oneota Cemetery in Duluth about a tall, shadowy figure and a specter dog that have been said to wander on occasion through the cemetery. The authors of this book learned of the legend thanks to a local man who told us his personal experience with the lengthy, thin ghost, which has come to be called the Tall Man.

According to his best recollection, the local was sixteen years old when he sighted the Tall Man during the fall of 1992. He and some daring friends had ventured into the old cemetery, which features gravestones dating as far back as the middle of the nineteenth century. The group of adolescents wanted to test their nerves and try to scare one another. In accordance with the storyteller's wishes, only his first name is mentioned.

As Jason remembers, once inside Oneota Cemetery, the teenagers found themselves widely dispersed from one another. Jason walked from gravestone to gravestone, reading the names and dates by the bright moonlight. It was no doubt a strange and lonely place to be.

No one in his group was familiar with the legend of the Tall Man. So when Jason heard one of his friends softly call, "Here comes someone," he assumed it was the cemetery caretaker out to run them off.

Jason hid, crouched behind a particularly large marker, and watched. The sixteen-year-old saw a lean, angular figure approach, led by a dog of medium height with a heavy build. The man and his dog strolled along an interior roadway designed to allow easy access into the cemetery.

As the duo drew closer to his hiding place, Jason heard what sounded like dog tags jingling. He and the others hunkered down, so they wouldn't be seen by what they believed was some responsible party. They were quite surprised when the lanky, dark figure and his dog strolled briskly past them and onward down the cemetery road. The man looked neither left nor right but marched smartly by at a steady pace, the dog mirroring its master precisely.

Jason imagined nothing supernatural until the two reached the point in the road where it made a sharp, ninety-degree turn. Straight ahead was a wall of heavy brush and trees, followed by a sheer drop-off of nearly a hundred feet. The turn, on the other hand, led back into the graveyard. To Jason's horror, the man and his dog walked straight into the brush. Crunching noises and footfalls were briefly heard, then there was only silence.

The encounter sent the teenagers running. Later, when the band of young friends reassembled and discussed what they had seen, they all agreed it was no living man or dog—and if they possibly might have been, they no longer were. Jason's earlier assessment had been that the caretaker was coming to send them away. It seems that they were right on both counts; maybe it was a former caretaker. Perhaps the man and dog were spectral beings, who once had walked the grounds as part of a job, and now were obliged to go on doing so beyond the grave.

The spirit of the Tall Man may wander the cemetery acting as a guardian with his trusty dog over the resting place of the deceased, watching for those who would intrude with a less than respectful attitude.

Further evidence of this comes from another local named Ethan. His story, from 1992, tells of a rowdy group of young people from Denfeld High School that were "hanging out" next to the cemetery with their car radio up loud. On the road that runs next to the cemetery, they saw the tall figure of a man approaching with a dog. Suddenly the dog broke away toward them at a run, snarling and showing its fangs. Without uttering a word, the man halted and raised his arm in a sweeping arc. Immediately, the summoned dog retreated and both of them turned and walked off the cliff's edge—just as Jason's group had witnessed. The boisterous crowd quickly turned somber at the eerie sight.

In Ethan's own words: "They walked directly down the impossibly steep embankment that was nothing but a cliff falling straight down a hundred feet into a creek bed."

Needless to say, the high schoolers took their party elsewhere in a hurry.

Though history does not provide us with a record of who this lonely man and his dog may have been, it seems likely that the ghost of the Tall Man and his loyal companion were bound together in life long ago, and continue on together as caretakers even after death. As they carry out their grim mission, they offer a lesson in humility, and respect for the strange and somber nature of cemeteries—and those who would guard them—assuring that all entombed there do indeed rest in peace.

Strange Creatures

MIDNIGHT WANDERER

*About midnight the thing came down through the forest
opposite, across the brook and stayed there on the hillside
for nearly an hour. They could hear the branches crackle
as it moved about, and several times it uttered a harsh,
guttural, long-drawn moan, a peculiarly sinister sound.*

—*Theodore Roosevelt,* The Wilderness Hunter

If you've ever spent a night alone in the woods and heard a
twig snap under the weight of some unknown animal, you will
know that a natural tenseness comes and wariness sets in.
Under these circumstances, even sounds that are well known
and understood become ominous and eerie. Coyotes sound
like demons, wolves like lost souls wandering the world, and
the scream of a bobcat like a woman being slowly tortured.

Once you've spent enough time in the wilderness, these
sounds become normal and even expected. That's why when
something completely unexpected and perhaps unnatural
occurs, you never forget it. Such is the case for me. A
big reason why the paranormal fascinates me is that I've
brushed against it on a few occasions. One of those times is
the subject of this story.

On a fall evening in 1990, I came home to a thick darkness.
My wife and young daughters were away visiting family.
It was a particularly quiet night, and the woods were still.
There was no wind and no moonlight. Something about the
calm and stillness made me uneasy. I sensed that I was not
alone. However, because I had worked all day and was tired,
I ignored my intuition.

I got out of the car and stepped toward our trailer home. Still,
the unsettling feeling did not leave me, so against my better
judgment, I decided to investigate. I ventured to the edge
of our yard and gazed deep into the shadows of the woods.
Suddenly, I heard it. The sound of approaching footsteps—
large, heavy footsteps—rose out of the darkness.

It was like nothing I had ever heard before, and it was

coming closer. Perhaps most disturbing to me was the slow deliberation with which it approached. In those first seconds of speculation, I imagined that it might be someone who was lost, trying to find their way home—an extremely unlikely scenario in my remote area. Nevertheless I called out, "Who's there?"

The footsteps stopped. The woods fell silent. A long moment passed with no response.

"Who's there?" I said, louder this time. Still there was no reply.

Fear began to creep upon me. Impulsively, I ran to the house, grabbed my shotgun and returned to the edge of the yard. Surprisingly, the weapon offered me little comfort. My sense of unease continued to grow.

I yelled once again, as loudly as I could, "Who's there?"

Silence.

Panic setting in, I lifted the shotgun, aimed high and fired into the air. In the impenetrable silence of the moment, the blast seemed deafening, but what followed was a noise that I would not believe had I not heard it myself. The creature roared. It bellowed from the very spot where the footfalls had ceased. It wailed at me for several seconds, its volume dwarfing the sound of my thunderous shotgun. The beast's wild, otherworldly siren call froze me in my tracks. Had it, in that instant, chosen to attack, I don't know what I would have done. Most probably, after soiling myself, I would have broken the land-speed record anywhere outside of the Utah salt flats.

Instead, it retreated at a dead run back in the direction from which it had come. I breathed a sigh of relief and relaxed, the tension leaving my body. But this ordeal wasn't over. The creature found its courage. Curiously and to my horror, it stopped running. It paused. Then it slowly began retracing its steps back in my direction.

I ask you now, what animal would possibly do this?

Without hesitation, I raised my shotgun and fired again. This time the behemoth retreated for good, snapping large sticks and twigs underfoot, pushing branches aside and breaking limbs from trees. The frightful sounds eventually faded from earshot. The creature was gone.

For a time, I stood paralyzed with dread. But at last, when the shock left me, I returned to the safety of my home. I called a friend not to tell him my story but just so I could hear a human voice. I needed to connect with someone familiar to calm my jangled nerves. And, yes, for the remainder of the night, I listened, edgy, to every approaching sound.

Before adding my story to this collection, I had only told it to a few trusted individuals: family members and close friends. However, this is a book about the remarkable, and if I'd never experienced the unexplainable, I probably wouldn't be writing it. So in the interest of honesty and because so many others bravely shared their own perplexing experiences, I decided that I must do the same. Besides, no book about the strange would be complete without a portion of it being devoted to the topic of Bigfoot.

MORE BIGFOOT SIGHTINGS

. . . talking about a yeti or bigfoot or sasquatch, I'm sure that they exist.

—Jane Goodall, 2002 National Public Radio interview

While some people are a bit unnerved at the thought of venturing into the wild, rugged country along the North Shore, many others savor the chance to get out and enjoy it. Such hardy souls are, by nature, practical people who are comfortable in the wilderness. They understand the world that surrounds them, or they wouldn't be out there.

Which explains why, when experienced woodsmen step forward to report run-ins with strange creatures, the sightings are hard to discount as either flights of fancy or honest cases of mistaken identity. Such woods-wise witnesses have substantial credibility. The persons involved in the following two accounts fall into this category.

On an unforgettable October day back in 1985, two grouse hunters reported a terrifying experience with an unexplainable creature in Lake County. The men were hunting near Lax Lake. Although the lake is not far from the city of Silver Bay, it's still a beautifully remote area.

As they hiked the heavily forested uplands in search of grouse, they occasionally heard the unmistakable sounds of a large animal following them. A curious bear, perhaps . . . or a rutting bull moose in search of female companionship?

It was disconcerting but not terribly threatening for the two well-armed hunters, who felt very much at home in their wild surroundings—until, as the shadows lengthened and daylight faded, the creature unleashed a thunderous howling sound. The men were petrified, but their ordeal didn't end there. They spotted the outline of an enormous two-legged creature standing in a nearby clearing, in the direction the sound had come from.

Though they survived the situation physically intact, it was an extremely frightening experience—one that no doubt lingers in their minds and stirs restless memories each time they venture into the northwoods.

A separate North Shore Bigfoot report, involving two men we'll call "Jim" and "Gary," also occurred in the Lake County region in the mid-'80s. The men made their livings primarily through logging and were well respected as honest, hard workers.

Jim and Gary were also experienced hunters and quite familiar with wolves, bears and the countless other animals that call northeastern Minnesota home. But what they saw is not something you'll find in the pages of a field guide.

As the story goes, the two men had ridden a dirt bike through the woods to a recent worksite to retrieve a skidder they needed at another logging operation.

They arrived at the jobsite without incident, but when Jim climbed aboard the battered skidder to fire up the engine and drive it out of the woods, he spotted something moving in a nearby clearing. He called to Gary to join him in the skidder's elevated cab for a better look—and what the men saw chilled them to the bone.

It is reported that they observed a huge, hair-covered creature striding purposefully across the small opening in the forest. The sight startled them so badly they abandoned the task at hand, climbed back on the dirt bike and fled. As the frightened men hastily sped away they spilled the bike. Gary was slightly injured, but the thought of the strange, hairy creature kept them moving.

Although that's the end of their story, I have to add that neither of these men impress me as the sort that would run from something they understood—or anything at all, for that matter.

Of course, reports like this stretch back into history. There have been stories of similarly strange sightings from all points of the globe. Whether you choose to believe them or not depends upon how you see the world. If it is a closed book—mapped and fully described by science with no corner unknown to us—then the rumored existence of Bigfoot can't possibly be true. However, new knowledge and new scientific discoveries come to us daily.

I'll admit that the likelihood of a living and breathing, gigantic, fur-covered "manimal" is fantastically unlikely—and scientifically unproven. For now, Bigfoot, Sasquatch, skunk-ape, missing link or whatever you want to call it lies squarely within the realm of the paranormal, much like ghosts, UFOs and the elusive Loch Ness Monster. But that doesn't mean it's not out there, an incredible creature of flesh and blood that is able to disappear at will. For all we know, conclusive evidence has already been unearthed and is about to be revealed to the world.

No one can know what the hunters outside Silver Bay saw or what frightened the loggers so. For that matter, no one can guess what countless other witnesses (including this author) have seen and heard over the years. Although there may be reasonable explanations for a creature that is both real and unreal, the answers remain in an uncharted corner of the universe—the domain of that which is said not to exist, but does.

WHAT'S IN THE LAKE?

There are giants in the sea . . .

—Michael Bright

Since mankind first dared to venture upon the water, legends have told of great monsters of the deep. Such stories are not limited to oceans. From Loch Ness to the Great Lakes, reports of mysterious creatures have circulated for centuries.

Lake Superior is no exception. Native legends, tales of the French voyageurs and modern shipping reports alike all provide accounts of strange beasts and frightening encounters.

One of the most well-known, modern-day lake monsters is *"Pressie"*—a creature reported to lurk in and around the Presque Isle River area north of Ironwood, Michigan, on the far eastern side of Lake Superior.

Pressie was first reported on Memorial Weekend in 1977. An Illinois man named Randy Braun claims to have had a terrifying experience with a giant serpent-like animal while beachcombing near the river mouth. First spotted at a distance of about 1,000 feet offshore, the creature quickly swam closer to shore—toward Braun. It was enormous, with the girth of a compact car, and had a horse-like head and whiskers.

The beast apparently became so curious about Mr. Braun that he was obliged to conceal himself behind a boulder on shore to evade further detection. Braun managed to snap a single, low-quality photograph of the creature before it moved off. Since Braun's initial report, other stories of encounters with a creature of similar description have emerged from that area of the lake.

Western Lake Superior has its share of strange sightings as well. For example, in 1897, a massive "serpent" reportedly attacked a man just offshore of Duluth. It happened after the man's yacht struck what was thought to be a rock. The "rock" turned out to be alive, and the creature apparently took exception to being put upon by the boat's hull. When the man fell from the vessel's deck into the water, the snake-like creature attempted to constrict him like a large boa. The witnesses—three horrified crew members—were petrified with fear and helpless to lend aid.

It is not documented whether or not the victim survived his terrifying encounter, but the attack offers a chilling account of an unidentified and extremely huge water beast haunting the waters of the North Shore.

Some 90 years later, in July of 1987, one of the lake's secrets was revealed to me. I was on my way to Two Harbors from Duluth, where I was working at the time. I came to an unpaved spot along Highway 61, next to the Stuart River. It was a great place to pull off in order to get a closer view of the lake and the river. It was also a wonderful spot for fishermen to cast a line, especially when the Kamloops rainbows are making their spawning runs up the river. I frequently stopped at this favorite location to stretch my legs and to get some fresh air.

The midsummer evening was hot and sticky, so the cool breeze blowing in from the lake felt like Heaven. I hoped to have the spot to myself for a few minutes, but I was disappointed to notice another car pull in behind me. It parked a discreet distance away, and a man wearing khaki shorts and an expensive-looking polo shirt hopped out, offering me a friendly wave.

The man spent a few minutes at the edge of a small cliff that rose twenty or thirty feet above the lake. I kept my distance from the stranger; I wasn't in the mood for company. However, much to my surprise, the man suddenly turned and walked straight toward me at a hurried pace. I considered retreating—a clear, nonverbal message that said, "Stay away"—but it was apparent that the stranger wanted to speak with me. I decided to be polite.

"Hello," said the man, then added a little sheepishly, "I don't mean to bother you, but do you know what kind of fish are in this lake?"

It was obvious to me that the middle-aged man was not

from the area—not surprising considering how many people travel to the North Shore of Lake Superior every summer, to experience the rare and relatively unspoiled beauty of this famous drive. The road is also a popular direct route to Canada.

"I don't know, all sorts I guess," I answered. "Where are you from?"

"I'm from Iowa—Cedar Rapids. I was just driving by, heading up to Thunder Bay for my job, and I thought I'd take in the view. But I saw something out there." He pointed in the direction of the lake, just beyond the mouth of the river. "There was this really big fish—or something—right out there."

He motioned to the spot once again. Then he led me to his perch, but the mysterious fish was nowhere in sight.

"I'm not what you'd call a fish expert," I said, now more than a bit intrigued. "But I do live nearby. What did it look like exactly?"

"I don't know," he said. "I guess it looked like a rock at first—or a turtle's back, maybe. It would submerge, and you could just make it out under the surface. Then it would move around and come back up."

"It might have been carp," I replied. "They bunch up together when they spawn. But I've never seen them here, and I don't think they spawn at this time of year."

"It wasn't carp," the man said too quickly.

He blushed and tried to compose himself, but I sensed his unease. The man wasn't telling me everything.

"You said it was big?" I asked encouragingly.

"Oh, yeah, it was pretty big." The man gestured, spreading his arms as wide as he could.

He still seemed embarrassed, almost apologetic—which was why I found it so easy to believe him.

"I've seen some strange things around these parts myself," I offered.

That seemed to reassure the man that I didn't think he was crazy. He spoke more confidently, saying, "Listen, I'm no Jacques Cousteau, but I've done quite a bit of fishing around the country. I'm a sales rep and I travel. So I've spent a fair amount of time on the water, and this was nothing I've ever seen before."

"Might have been an otter," I suggested.

"No, I've seen otters and beavers before. This was bigger and I never saw the head…" The stranger stopped talking, as if trying to decide whether to share his final secret. Whatever he had seen had certainly affected the man.

"What is it?" I asked.

"You could tell," he began in a confidential tone. "There was more of it under the surface. Like the tip of an iceberg . . . the water is really clear. The last time it submerged, it moved really fast. Its dark, shiny back went under, and it actually created a small wake. And it was gone."

"That sounds pretty strange," I confessed, then chuckled nervously. "Who knows? The lake is sort of connected to the ocean. There could be anything out there, I guess."

The man looked at his watch, then back at me. He smiled sheepishly and said, "Probably a big turtle or something. Thanks for your time." And he left.

I never quite knew what to make of the man's story, but I found it unsettling. I even stopped scuba diving for a while. Still, old habits die hard. As the weeks passed, the sighting seemed a little less scary, and before summer was over I was back in the water again.

Once, I even dove near the spot the man reported seeing the strange creature. Though I kept an extra-sharp watch, I never spotted anything unusual. Yet I did note that a powerful current parallels the shoreline at that point. Whether that attracted the creature or held up its journey for a few brief moments, no one can say.

To this day, I wonder whether the man was seeing things or

if he witnessed one of the big lake's strangest inhabitants. His description of how the creature's shiny back surfaced and moved all but eliminates the possibility it was a log or giant turtle. The sheer size seems to rule out even the largest lake trout or sturgeon. And then there was the man's demeanor—honest, almost apologetic, even shaken—in a word, believable.

In the end we can never know exactly what surfaced off the Stuart River that day. Yet anyone with an open mind, anyone who is willing to believe in the paranormal, can certainly admit: Anything is possible on the mysterious North Shore of Lake Superior.

THE WOLF'S EYE

Dark eyes so grim, claws gleaming in the air, set to rip, to stab, to tear.

—*Kathryn Lasky, from her Guardians of Ga'Hoole series, book three,* The Rescue

If you imagine Lake Superior as the silhouette of a wolf's head, then Isle Royale is its eye. As the lake's largest island, Isle Royale measures forty-five miles long and nine miles wide. Now part of the Isle Royale National Park—an archipelago comprised of more than 450 islands—it is accessible only by boat or seaplane.

Within the park, visitors must explore afoot or afloat, as wheeled vehicles are prohibited. Such limited traffic and other regulations have helped the island return to a semblance of its formerly wild state. Though its lasting, untamed nature persists—it is not an untouched, pristine wilderness. And its rugged landscape holds countless secrets of human struggles dating back hundreds, even thousands of years.

The earliest visitors—indigenous peoples seeking copper from the island's rich mineral deposits—arrived perhaps 5,000 years ago. As Europeans explored the Great Lakes region, the French mapped and named the island. Later, its control moved to British hands. Benjamin Franklin bargained Isle Royale into U.S. territory in 1783, and European copper miners, commercial fishermen and loggers sought its riches throughout the 1800s. The Anishinabe (Ojibwe) people lost control of the island in 1843, when it officially became part of the United States. The early 1900s were the island's resort era, as large steamships ferried in summer tourists with their linen suits and parasols. In 1940, it was established as a national park and has since become a shining example of nature's ability to heal the scars of human abuses.

Looking back over Isle Royale's history, one of the strangest and most terrifying stories stems from the 1930s. At the time, the island was home to a logging camp of the Mead Lumber Company. The men shared the island with a uniquely limited variety of animal species. Moose arrived on the island around the year 1900, perhaps swimming from the Canadian shore. Fifty years later, wolves came to the island by crossing an uncommon ice bridge over the lake. Relatively few other animal species could be found on Isle Royale—except for those that flew. Needless to say, food for the island's inhabitants could become scarce, especially in the winter.

The lumberjacks who chose to make a living on Isle Royale were incredibly isolated. While the island's rugged beauty no doubt provided some consolation, they endured spans of weeks and even months away from anywhere that felt like home. They worked long hours and tolerated stretches of loneliness for the sake of a paycheck. Even if they wanted to leave, they were often trapped. The ice-ridden waters that surrounded Isle Royale frequently prohibited boats to dock for months at a time. That's why when trouble struck on the evening of January 3, 1936, the situation was so dire.

On that dark winter night, two employees of the Mead Lumber Company were charged with the task of collecting wood from the nearby woodpile. One of the men, Arthur Ruokenen, was just twenty-two years old. He wore his customary fur cap—a common head covering for a man of the woods to have fashioned. It kept him warm and staved off the biting winds of a cold, Lake Superior winter. However, as Ruokenen soon learned, wearing his cap on that night was a fateful mistake.

The two lumberjacks were used to the ways of the woods, and were not easily alarmed by wild creatures moving about. Even so, they most certainly kept watchful lookouts to all sides. Unfortunately they never expected their attacker to descend from above.

Seemingly from out of nowhere, a great horned owl swooped down upon them. Standing two feet tall, with a wingspan of up to sixty inches, the merciless raptor—sometimes called the "Meat Hook" or "Flying Tiger"—is a formidable opponent. Its soft, fleece-like feathers deadened the sound of air rushing over its wings, allowing it to drop in noiselessly on its unsuspecting prey. The bird's talons spread wide as it pounced onto the first man, slicing him across the head.

They had little time to wonder why the creature had attacked, for when it reached toward Ruokenen's fur cap, the answer was apparent. The owl was simply searching for a meal, and Ruokenen's headpiece was an excellent imitation of its prey.

Ruokenen couldn't react quickly enough. The predator curled its great talons and squeezed with the force necessary to disable a small mammal—hoping to grasp it and carry it away. Unfortunately for Ruokenen, the great owl's talons scratched one of his eyes and pierced the other most horribly.

The two men screamed in agony and terror. A third man nearby heard their cries and rushed to their rescue. As he dashed onto the scene, he recognized the situation and prudently threw a blanket over his head for protection. Skillfully swinging his axe, he killed the owl and ended the bizarre attack.

The Coast Guard was immediately called, and the cutter *Crawford* was dispatched from Duluth. However, due to difficult waters, she wasn't able to reach Ruokenen for more than twenty-four hours. Furthermore, news reports stated that, as the *Crawford* hurried Ruokenen back to the mainland, she battled ice floes and treacherous waters.

From the National Archives and Records in Washington, D.C., the *Crawford's* daily logbook confirms the radio call for assistance on the island, and the rescue of the lumberman. Finally, just before noon on January 5, Ruokenen was delivered to St. Luke's Hospital in Duluth. And there, this story ends. We know that Ruokenen's left eye was totally destroyed and that there was at least some hope of saving his eyesight in the one remaining eye. We also know that the owl was later dissected and found to have a completely empty stomach, verifying the reason for its unusual attack. However, there is no further record of what became of Arthur Ruokenen.

Perhaps Ruokenen was like so many other young, Finnish men who simply passed through the area, following the work, as area after area was logged and mined. Or maybe he stayed in Duluth but never had a wife or child with whom to leave his mark behind. He might even have returned to Isle Royale—only to witness the summer forest fire of 1936 roar out of the Mead Lumber Company's slash piles. Perhaps Ruokenen withdrew from the island for good when the company closed its operation before the end of the year. We cannot say for certain where fate brought the survivor of the desperate owl's brutal assault, but we can assure you that this is one encounter with the wild that will live in infamy amid the many strange and bizarre tales of the mysterious North Shore.

Water, Waves and Boats

THE LUCKY BELLE

Fortune favors the bold.

—Terence, 190-159 BC

Ships are made to travel. From bow to stern, from hatch covers to anchor—and every part in between—it's what they do. By nature and design they are always bound for another port, which is perhaps what draws us to think about them.

We wonder where they were built, how they were named and what their sometimes enormous dimensions might be. We are curious about the interesting things that might have happened aboard in years past or even what the people working now might be doing. But most of all, we wonder where they are going and where they have been.

It matters little whether the vessel is a mighty oceangoing vagabond or an ordinary old tug whose path and cargo are constant and predictable. Ships are interesting. We might even entertain romantic thoughts about whether a ship might possess an innate urge to roam, a desire woven into the very timbers or steel of its hull.

And why not? We name ships and baptize them like they are people. Isn't it possible for an exceptional boat to be born under a wandering, if not lucky, star?

One vessel that offers an interesting tale of luck and wanderlust—even after being dismembered—is the *Belle P. Cross*. If there is such a thing as a "lucky" shipwreck, the *Cross* experienced it. Having just been rebuilt after a fire, she was Lake Superior's first recorded accident of the 1903 season.

According to the Minnesota Department of Natural Resources' Division of Parks and Recreation, the 153-foot steam barge was en route from Two Island River to Duluth, her cargo consisting of railroad ties and timber. Unfortunately, on April 29 the ship and her crew found themselves caught in a blinding snowstorm.

Official accounts tell us that her captain saw lights on a

logging dock at the Gooseberry River and mistook them for another vessel at sea. Supposedly, the captain assumed from the lights that he was a safe distance from land and veered toward them—crashing his ship directly into shore.

We find this account difficult to believe. While history tells us that the ship was driven ashore, we cannot imagine a captain steering into the path of an oncoming vessel under any circumstances. Therefore, we pose an alternate hypothesis that seems to make more sense.

As the *Cross* headed toward Duluth, she was continuously pushed toward the shoreline by wind and waves. When the captain saw the lighted dock, he realized just how close to land he was. He also realized what a terrible dilemma he now faced. If he stayed his course, he would drive the ship straight into the volcanic rocks that treacherously jutted out from the sea—almost certainly sinking the vessel and killing his crew. If he turned to the left, he would put the ship broadside into the prevailing sea, where a rogue wave could easily swamp the *Cross* or push her directly into the high rocks. His only alternative was a starboard turn—toward land and to a place known for its gravel beach.

We cannot know for certain what the captain's intentions were, but we do know that fortune favored him and his crew. With unbelievable good luck, the *Cross* struck land and came promptly to rest against the lumber camp dock. All eighteen crew members stepped out of the barge, onto the dock and strolled safely to shore. Who could calculate the odds of crashing a ship in a raging blizzard and safely reaching a dock without so much as getting one's feet wet?

The *Cross* herself wasn't quite as lucky. The thirty-four-year-old wooden steamer was discharged of her most valuable freight, then torn apart by huge rollers. Worse yet, according to reports of the wreck from the *Buffalo Evening News* and *Port Huron Daily Times*, she was valued at $14,000 but carried no insurance.

The stricken *Cross* was salvaged in short order, and her boiler, engine and various body parts were unceremoniously dissected and sold. When the vultures had finished picking her apart, all that remained was her anchor—and only because the mighty hook was more trouble to move than it was worth.

Weighing roughly 1,500 pounds, the unwieldy hunk of metal remained, rusting away as a grim reminder of Lake Superior's fury. When Gooseberry Falls State Park opened in the 1920s, the anchor became a favorite nautical prop for visitors carrying cameras.

Then on a late night in the 1940s, a group of rambunctious young men got the wild idea to take the anchor for a ride. How they lifted the solid mass of metal onto their truck is a mystery of its own. Before the lads reached their destination, their truck gave out under the strain of the huge anchor and they had to dump their ill-gotten cargo in the woods.

As the story goes, the boys had big plans to return and retrieve their prize the following day. But cooler heads prevailed and several years passed before they went back as men to collect their pirated treasure. The land where the anchor rested had changed hands since the heist, however, and the new owner refused to let them take it. Apparently, the woman who owned the property enjoyed her new lawn ornament, claiming that it lent originality to her flower garden.

Decades later, the grown son of one of the original heist men was allowed to move the anchor back to the shoreline of Gooseberry Park. And with his own backhoe and truck, he did just that. It now rests within sight of the water, and an interpretive sign is soon to be installed—a small bookmark to this weighty piece of history.

A rugged mass of metal is the last piece of evidence to a tale of incredible providence. It was a stroke of fate in the teeth of a raging storm that brought the little ship more neatly to harbor than the best laid plan might have. What a happy accident that the *Belle P. Cross* could discharge her passengers on dry land, moments before she broke apart past all repair. She may have been ruined in the trying, but the *"Lucky Belle"* performed her final job admirably.

RAPTURE OF THE DEEP

Mariners have paid a substantial price in attempting to master the big lake.

—*Julius F. Wolff, Jr.,* Lake Superior Shipwrecks

Who among us hasn't fantasized about finding buried treasure? Who doesn't dream of striking it rich through research, hard work, dedication and a lot of luck? Of course, we all do, but what would we be willing to risk for it? Would we dare to put our lives, financial security and reputations in jeopardy in an endless pursuit of a dream? Most of us wouldn't. However, for some people—like the men in this story—the answer is yes.

The saga began nearly a century ago, with an unfortunate lesson in the wages of greed and the true cost of cutting too many corners. It stretches to this day, as one man's obsession continues to fuel a passionate quest for one of Lake Superior's greatest treasures.

As with nearly every large body of water on the planet, Lake Superior holds amazing riches within her depths. One of her most notorious jewels is the luxury yacht *Gunilda*. Owned by William Harkness, a wealthy and arrogant oil barren of Standard Oil fame, the *Gunilda* was the flagship of the New York Yacht Club shortly after the turn of the century.

At one hundred ninety-five feet in length, with ornate mahogany trim and gold scrollwork accenting her spotless white hull, the steam-driven vessel was a sight to behold. Towering twin masts and a huge stack amidships further enhanced her regal appearance.

Built in Scotland in 1897, the *Gunilda's* steel hull could slice through the waves at fourteen knots, thanks to her massive steam engine and twin boilers. In the summer of 1911, she steamed through the Great Lakes toward the far corners of Lake Superior, as Harkness entertained family and friends on an almost decadent cruise.

The ship's untimely demise came on August 29, about five miles outside of Rossport, Ontario. Ever the shrewd businessman, Harkness had balked at the price a local pilot had requested to guide the *Gunilda* through the channels and rocks in this part of the lake. Apparently, Harkness considered the man's fifteen-dollar fee an exorbitant amount for safe passage, so he ordered his crew of twenty to "carry on" toward Rossport without a guide.

Shortly thereafter, the ship rammed McGarvey Shoal. The force drove her elegant bow high onto the rock, while the rest of the ship floated precariously over Superior's icy depths. Harkness sent for a powerful tugboat—the *James Whelan*—to free the *Gunilda*. When the tug arrived with the barge *Empire* in tow, its captain strongly recommended using a second barge to form a sling around the *Gunilda's* hull so she wouldn't sink.

Again, Harkness balked at what he considered an unreasonable and unnecessary cost. He ordered the *James Whelan* to pull her free, saying, "She went straight on, she'll come straight off!" And so she did, before keeling to starboard, filling with water and sinking in more than two hundred feet of water.

Fortunately, no lives were lost that day. Harkness and his entourage reportedly boarded the next available train and returned to New York City. Apparently, the oil baron was content simply to accept his insurance money and move on with his life. He never made any attempts at salvaging his yacht. Instead he left behind a pristine ship fitted with fine mahogany and stocked with the best French wines, china and ornate furnishings that money could buy. The ship even held a piano and complete music room. Most certainly, Harkness was at least somewhat embarrassed by the results of his rash decisions, and whether or not he took to sea again is unknown.

There is no doubt that word spread quickly of this treasure waiting to be claimed at the bottom of the lake. It was a ticket to life on easy street for whoever could find the *Gunilda* and raise her. But she was too deep. The dive technology needed—including compressed air tanks with modern regulators—did not yet exist. It would be more than fifty years before a legitimate salvage attempt was made, and that effort was a colossal failure. It succeeded only in breaking the *Gunilda's* mast and sending her fifty feet deeper into the lake.

In the summer of 1970, two new players entered the story. Fred Broennle and Charles "King" Hague, both of Thunder Bay, began their own zealous quest to discover the *Gunilda*—dreaming of the riches she would bring them. They made a pact to find the legendary boat together and to share her hoards of wealth.

In an exclusive interview with us in 2007, Fred Broennle shared the details of their tragic misadventures.

Both men were aware that this would be a dangerous endeavor. Hague, by far the more experienced diver, taught Broennle everything he could about deep, technical diving. In Lake Superior's cold waters, dives of this nature were especially challenging and dangerous, requiring a combination of mixed gases and heavy-duty gear.

Even with the best of equipment, divers couldn't descend farther than 200 feet below sea level for more than a few minutes at a time. To do so increased the likelihood of developing a condition known as "nitrogen narcosis," which resulted in significantly decreased cognitive skills and severely impaired judgment—a deadly combination. Described by legendary undersea explorer Jacques Cousteau as "rapture of the deep," nitrogen narcosis had been the cause of death for countless divers, some of whom went so far as to remove their breathing regulators from their mouths, divest themselves of their air tanks and attempt to swim like fish.

Extensive preparation brought Broennle and Hague to one fateful August day. With only a rough idea of where the *Gunilda* lay, the duo began making reconnaissance dives in search of the missing treasure. At first, Broennle was enthusiastic and eager to partake in such a thrilling adventure. But as the day progressed, he began to worry. His instincts told him that Hague and he were pushing too hard. They were diving too often with too little time to rest and recover in between.

Soon Broennle began to suspect that Hague was experiencing symptoms of nitrogen narcosis: disorientation and mental confusion. The younger diver suggested that they call it a day or least take a break for a few hours, but Hague was determined to make yet another dive. Broennle begged him to reconsider, and when he wouldn't listen, Broennle decided to dive with his mentor in order to ensure his safety. Broennle asked Hague to wait while he suited up, but impatience won the day. Hague immediately dropped from the side of the boat like a dead weight.

Knowing that he would never be able to catch up with his friend, Broennle waited inside the boat. He was relieved to see a steady stream of bubbles rising from Hague's location. It was a sign that everything was going well below the surface. But soon the steady stream turned into intermittent clusters of bubbles, signifying that trouble was lurking. Within minutes the bubbles stopped altogether.

Broennle checked his watch and made a horrifying realization: By now, Hague had to be out of air. When Hague's dive light bobbed to the surface, Broennle's worst fears were all but confirmed.

Broennle became panicky with despair, and he resolved to reach his friend no matter the cost. He dropped into the water, plummeting fast. Overwhelmed with confusion and grief, Broennle didn't take the proper precautions. Too late, he tried to fill his buoyancy control device to slow his descent, but his efforts failed.

He grappled for a hold on the shoal but lost his grip and continued to fall, bouncing off the rock face like a toy. He felt consciousness slipping away from him, when he suddenly landed with a thud. Broennle opened his eyes to discover that he was at the bottom of Lake Superior, 280 feet below the surface. And there, next to him, lay the gold-leafed bowsprit of the *Gunilda*. They had found the lost yacht.

Broennle was instantly beguiled and enchanted, but he also realized through his fogged brain that he was quickly running out of air. He started to climb out of the abyss, hand over hand up the jagged rock, but time worked against him.

Fifty feet from the surface Broennle lost consciousness. For most, that would spell doom. However, Lake Superior had decided that one lost life was enough for the day. Broennle's buoyancy control device carried him to the surface and to the fresh air that he so desperately needed. When the young man awakened, he vowed to one day bring his friend's body back to the surface for a proper burial.

Six years passed before Broennle was able to fulfill his promise. He returned to the doomed ship with a submersible camera. As he sent it down for a look at the yacht, the sea scanner became entangled in the port side stays. He managed to work the camera loose by repeatedly panning and tilting it. Eventually it broke free and fell to the bottom.

Broennle glanced at the viewing screen and saw a sight that chilled him to the bone. There, as clear as could be, was a pair of swim fins—Hague's swim fins. The camera had settled next to the body of his friend, who was resting with the *Gunilda's* flagstaff mysteriously across his chest. Even after so many years of submersion, the features of Hague's face were clearly recognizable, preserved by the dark, freezing water. Broennle was overcome with grief as his friend's body was brought to the surface.

Though it can never be known for certain, one can most likely surmise that Hague's death was caused by rapture of the deep. After making several dives previous to the one that ended his life, he was tired and feeling the effects of clouded judgment. By the time he reached the *Gunilda*, his cognitive skills were probably worse than they would have been for someone who was legally intoxicated. His reflexes were slowed, and he felt a euphoric giddiness, as well as fearlessness. He would have considered himself invulnerable and would have ignored signs of danger and distress until the very end.

Sadly, Hague was not the only diver who lost his life in an attempt to reach the *Gunilda*. In 1989, Reg Barrett of Burlington, Ontario, suffered a similar fate—another comrade lost to rapture of the deep.

Broennle nearly lost his life on the day that Hague died. Instead, he survived and gained a new obsession. The diver was bewitched by the sight of the *Gunilda's* pristine, white bow with her intricate golden scrollwork. Raising the yacht became his love, his life's mission.

"If you can imagine the most beautiful, sensual woman," Broennle told us, "that is the *Gunilda*. Don't call it a wreck; she's just moored down there."

His tireless efforts on behalf of the boat left him exhausted mentally, emotionally and financially. He spent endless hours and burned through all of his resources in a vain attempt to call the *Gunilda* his own. Broennle made three separate trips to Lloyd's of London in England in order to obtain exclusive salvage rights, and he still maintains that he holds a legal claim to the yacht.

We should not judge Fred Broennle's obsession too harshly. After all, how many of us can say that we've truly followed our dreams? Broennle himself acknowledges, "A lot of people say I'm crazy, but I'd do it all over again in a New York minute."

He bucked a society that expects and requires us to live our lives a certain way and to practice the norms of our culture. Instead, he followed his heart and says that he has but one regret in life: losing his friend and teacher King Hague. While the path Broennle chose may not be for all of us, we must applaud his courage and dedication.

And we cannot fault him for his obsession. After all, even the Cousteau team, on an exploratory trip to Lake Superior in 1980, proclaimed the *Gunilda* to be "the most beautiful wreck in the world."

RING OF HOPE

Those grand fresh-water seas of ours . . .
Are swept by Borean and dismasting blasts
As direful as any that lash the salted wave;
they know what shipwrecks are, for out of sight
of land, however inland, they have drowned full
many a midnight ship with all its
shrieking crew.

—*Herman Melville,* Moby Dick

On December 6, 1927, the 250-foot freighter *Kamloops* was making her last voyage of the season. As she steamed up the lake from the Soo Locks of Michigan toward Fort William, Ontario, no one could have known it was to be her last voyage ever.

She was much like her hard-working sister vessels that tramped the ocean and was built to carry cargo of every description except for coal and ore. After three years as a package freighter, often carrying passengers, the *Kamloops* now followed the Canadian steamer *Quedoc*. This trip was made many times by both boats, and was all in a day's work.

There was nothing unusual about that day's passage, except that Captain Bill Brian, master of the *Kamloops*, had already waited three days in the face of a northerly gale. The storm had finally abated, but Captain Brian couldn't have guessed that the worst was yet to come.

By the time the sun set on the two ships and their crews, winds were blowing at near hurricane force and the thermometer stood at thirty degrees below zero. The nineteen men and two women aboard the *Kamloops* found themselves in the most dangerous of waters. To make matters worse, they were approaching Isle Royale. Even in the calmest of seas, Isle Royale's many reefs and rocks posed a formidable challenge. Captain Brian was a seasoned navigator, yet in those mounting conditions, his years of experience and familiarity with the sea's hidden dangers did him little good. Up ahead lay timeless rocks, mightier than steel, waiting beneath the waves.

That night the Kamloops' powerful steam engine was like a clock, with every piston stroke ticking through the eleventh hour and toward a place called Twelve O'clock Point, a place that would come to be well known in the maritime history of the Great Lakes. You must understand, dear reader, that on this particular night in December of 1927 the Great Lake would not only flex her muscle, she would become pitiless in her rage. William Rattigan paints a painfully accurate picture of a Superior storm in his book, *Great Lakes: Shipwrecks and Survivals.*

"Storms exploding across hundreds of miles of open water pile up mountainous seas that strike swifter and more often than the deadliest waves on any ocean."

With the *Quedoc* in the lead, the two ships kept each other in sight as they struggled through the near-blinding winter storm. As the *Quedoc* attempted to "thread the needle," passing between the northeast tip of Isle Royale and Passage Island, she suddenly veered to avoid a mass of rock that had appeared in the dense night. Sounding her warning whistle, as though in final salute, the *Quedoc* lost sight of the *Kamloops* in the thickening storm.

What happened to the *Kamloops* after losing visual contact with the *Quedoc* is something of a mystery. However, most likely, the unfortunate ship was ripped and ravaged some time between 10 p.m. and daybreak by the giant lake and the menacing rocks that surround Isle Royale. The damage sustained was enough to send the *Kamloops* to the bottom in a matter of minutes.

Most of the crew died in the water, either by way of drowning or crashing against the jagged rocks. But according to longtime Isle Royale fisherman Milford Johnson (who was then just a boy) and corroborated by well-known game warden Jack Linklater, seven people made it to land. How they got ashore on a night like that—the ship grinding and tearing on the rocks, the wind turning every drop of water to ice, the rough seas making a swim to safety nearly impossible—we can hardly imagine. Nevertheless, most reliable accounts have six men and one woman reaching shore at Twelve O'clock Point. Apparently through incredible luck and a phenomenal will to live, they struggled to shore, found each other and huddled together for warmth.

Soaked to the bone in temperatures well below zero, there was little they could do—but they did their best. Some attempted to get a fire started while others built a crude shelter, a lean-to of driftwood and brush. Whether or not that fire ever came to life is not known, though it seems unlikely. But the very fact that they got as far as they did is a remarkable testament to their courage and will to live.

Even if they had successfully gotten the fire ablaze, it probably would not have helped. They were no doubt nearly frozen to death already. The seven of them formed a small circle around their last hope of warmth and salvation. Perhaps they even prayed that the wind would die down and the fire would come up. It seems, though, that those prayers were not answered.

Hypothermia slowed their limbs and finally their minds. Each of the seven in turn, sitting around a lifeless fire pit beneath a crude shelter, slipped away. We can only imagine their final moments before endless sleep overtook them. One of them, the ship's mate, reached into his pocket and withdrew a small piece of candy. Maybe he planned to put it in his mouth but never quite got it there. Or perhaps he intentionally kept it between his thumb and fingers, a tiny metaphor for whomever found his body. The piece of candy was shaped like a little ring buoy—a Lifesaver.

It wasn't until spring of 1928, as the warm sun drew forth new green leaves to the branches, that Johnson and Linklater found the small group. They were still sitting upright, frozen as hard as marble statues, insulated under their shelter as they had been all winter long. The ship's mate still clutched his Lifesaver.

Fifty years after the sinking of the *Kamloops*, her wreckage was discovered in two hundred feet of water off Twelve O'clock Point, on the northeast side of Isle Royale. Despite this find, much of the history surrounding this tragedy is unknown to us. Most notably, we will never understand exactly how seven courageous people managed to make their way ashore that night—a night when the wind, the water and the weather all seemed to conspire against them.

Truth is stranger than fiction, and in this case the truth is more heroic and poignant as well. Much of history is unknown to us, but in searching for the answers we discovered something about ourselves: Our lives are precious and worth fighting for. In the dark, cold waters of Lake Superior, too deep for most divers to venture, the *Kamloops* rests, along with some of the people who took that ill-fated last ride with her. Lake Superior will keep them, and we will remember them.

It's also worth noting that while researching this story, we were a bit skeptical about the ironic image of the ship's mate and the Lifesaver candy. It seemed a little too much like the embellishment of a storyteller's imagination. However, we felt a chill sweep through us when reviewing recent underwater photographs of the *Kamloops* wreck. In one stroke the events from long ago leapt to life through a single image. One of them clearly and hauntingly shows an open, wooden crate containing row after row of neatly wrapped Pep-o-mint Lifesavers.

STORM OF THE AGES

It has been a week that will always be remembered. It has been a week that children of today will tell their children and their children's children about years hence. Fortunately, even grim old Lake Superior is seldom seen in such rage, and nor within the memory of living men has one of her furies resulted in such appalling disasters.

—Duluth Evening Herald, *December 2, 1905*

Huddled together in watchful anxiety, forty thousand pairs of eyes peered through the slashing snow, trying to determine whether any part of the ship remained above water. Half the town of Duluth had gathered on the shores of Minnesota Point during the night of November 27, 1905, riveted by the horrific scene and utterly helpless to lend aid.

Off the coast, in only seventeen feet of water, the 430-foot steel bulk freighter *Mataafa* lay broken in three pieces. The once magnificent ship was just a few hundred feet from onlookers, but the distance might as well have been ten miles. Winds whipped at sixty to eighty miles per hour, and the temperature began its perilous drop to thirteen degrees below zero. No rescue boat could navigate the lake's pounding waves. The *Mataafa* and her crew were trapped in a storm that would wreck thirty ships and claim thirty-six lives throughout the Great Lakes.

An elderly Duluth woman shared with us her grandfather's memories. He had been among the many anxious citizens that night.

This is what she said: "My grandfather went down to Park Point as soon as he heard about the ship in trouble. He went to see what he could do to help. They were all down there, lots of people, thousands of them, trying to figure out some ways to get those people off the ship. But there just wasn't any way to get to them, you know. They were close, really close, but the waves were too big."

At the turn of the 20th century, Duluth was one of the busiest ports in the world. It also had a reputation as one of the Great Lakes' most dangerous, due to its frequent, unforgiving storms. However, it was also the conventional understanding that a November storm would be followed by three to seven days of calm, as typical pressure patterns emerged. Therefore, after the vicious storm on November 23 through 25, it is understandable why ships headed out of ports across the Great Lakes, believing that the coast was clear.

Thinking the same, Captain Robert Humble of the *Mataafa* left the safety of Duluth's harbor, towing the consort barge *James Nasmyth*, on the afternoon of November 27. The sea greeted him with the escalating winds of a nor'easter; the week's second major storm was upon them.

Captain Humble and his crew spent ten hours with engines at full steam, but they could make little headway into the face of the gale. Outside Two Harbors, less than twenty miles from Duluth, the captain made a dicey decision: He gave the order to put about. Such a maneuver was almost never attempted, except in the direst of circumstances. It would expose the ship's broadside to a lashing of waves, any one of which could capsize the freighter. Success would require nerves of steel, tremendous skill and more than a little luck.

Surprisingly, Humble's gamble paid off. He made the turn, bringing both the *Mataafa* and the *Nasmyth* safely about. Now he could run back to the safety of Duluth's harbor, with the violent winds at his back.

When Humble once again reached the port city, he faced another terrible decision. He knew that he could not make it through the new piers' entrance with both boats, so he gave the order to cut the *Nasmyth* free. It is not a decision the captain would have made lightly, as the odds would have been against the smaller barge. However, incredibly, the *Nasmyth* let down her anchors and held fast throughout the storm, preserving cargo and crew. As for the unfortunate *Mataafa*, the last hurdle between her crew and safety was a maneuver nearly as difficult as the miraculous turn accomplished outside Two Harbors.

The Duluth ship canal, as you see it today, had only recently been completed in 1905. It consisted of two concrete breakwaters that extended several hundred feet from under the Aerial Lift Bridge out into Lake Superior. The *Mataafa* attempted to make her way between the narrow opening at the end of those piers. Amazingly, the remarkable feat would have been accomplished if not for a series of untimely waves. Aided by the unrelenting gale force winds, the waves slammed the *Mataafa* into the north pier just as her bow had entered that small sliver of hope. Helplessly, the freighter was swept back into the open sea. She was spun like a top in the raging storm and driven into the south pier. Her back nearly broken, the *Mataafa* was pushed northwest of the piers where she was driven to ground and came to rest.

For the remainder of the night, the ship was unreachable and the crowd from shore kept vigil. She was pounded by unrelenting waves and endured subzero temperatures. Finally, late in the morning on November 28, the Coast Guard was able to get a lifeboat alongside her. In the forward end they found some of the crew still clinging to life. Many of them had spent the night in the captain's cabin and had built a fire in his bathtub, scavenging wood from furniture and tearing away wall paneling to stoke the blaze.

In the stern section, nine crewmen were found, but none of them had survived. Without fire and with no shelter from the furious gale, they had all died of exposure. The engineer's body was recovered from a sheath of ice that had encased him like a mummy. To remove his body from the scene, workers needed to chop him free from the ship's icy grip.

Our elderly storyteller added, "After it was all over, the next day, Grandfather brought home a section of a rosary. They were beads that he and others down at the beach used to pray the rosary together by the fire. There was nothing else they could do for those people. When he came home, he gave those beads to his wife, my grandmother. And every day of her life, she would say a prayer for those poor people who were lost on that ship, every day until she died at ninety. I remember seeing those dark beads shining at her waistline, attached to the belt of her dress. There they were every single day, and she was buried wearing them."

In the spring of 1906, the *Mataafa* was at last pulled free from her resting place just off the shore of what is now Canal Park. Despite the lives lost in that ill-fated attempt to thread the needle to safe harbor she was put back together, refitted and was again plying the waters of the Great Lakes before the 1906 season had ended. Beyond the romance and occasional tragedy involved in the shipping business, it is just that: a business. She remained a sturdy, working ship well into the 1960s when she was finally scrapped—an unceremonious end to a vessel with such a storied past.

The *Mataafa* may have survived long after that storm of the ages, but for some of her crew, luck and life came to an end aboard the frozen wreck. The wind carried away their breaths and the cold stilled their hearts—all just a stone's throw away from the warmth and safety of dry land.

THE STARVING MOON

*. . . I cannot say what excessive Hunger might do, which is
now their Case, the Ground being all cover'd with snow . . .*

—Daniel Defoe, Robinson Crusoe

Each year, countless visitors marvel at the North Shore's
rugged beauty. Many dream of spending time, if not settling
down, in such a wild and scenic environment. Yet few who
entertain these romantic dreams can imagine what life
would be like if they were trapped in a remote corner of the
wilderness. Or how quickly the area's beloved primeval spirit
could be transformed into a cruel and unforgiving master
when the surroundings became a prison from which there
was little hope of escape.

That is exactly what happened to Angelique Mott in the
winter of 1843. Betrayed by their employers, she and her
husband, Charlie, were trapped on a small island in the
majestic and isolated archipelago of Isle Royale. Her story
creates a gripping tableau of a few brutal months, shining
a bright light on Angelique's fortitude and, for her man,
unconquerable trials.

The only reliable account we have about her harrowing
experience comes from a solitary interview found in the
footnotes of the book *The Honorable Peter White*. After
spending hours of research time in libraries, museums
and historical societies across three states, we could shed
precious little light on Angelique.

The one document that did appear was at Isle Royale
National Park. A copy of a marriage certificate, for a Catholic
ceremony performed by the renowned Father Baraga at
LaPointe, Madeline Island, Wisconsin in 1842. The record
shows that Angelique was 19 at that time and Charlie 31
years of age. We have nothing else to substantiate this
following rousing report made by a remarkable woman, if
she does say so herself.

Described as "free-limbed, full grown and possessed of

enormous strength," she was of Anishinabe descent and apparently had boundless physical endurance. A story circulated that she once wagered a Frenchman that she could haul a barrel of port to the top of a hill and back. Winning with ease, she is said to have then volunteered to carry the barrel up again—with the Frenchman riding atop it! Whether this colorful tale of her haughty spirit ever really transpired is unknown, but she certainly had a reputation as an incredibly capable and strangely powerful creature.

Three years after she became a married woman, she and her husband traveled to Isle Royal on the schooner Algonquin, with the group of speculators prospecting for copper. We'll let her tell you about it.

". . . I wandered a long way on the beach until I saw something shining in the water. It was a piece of mass copper. When I told [the prospecting investors] of it they were very glad and determined at once to locate it. They said if Charlie and I would occupy it for them, Charlie should have $25 a month and I $5 to cook for him."

Although Isle Royale would eventually yield more than 95 million pounds of copper, she and Charlie would reap few of the rewards. They did strike the bargain to guard the claim for the wealthy men. Angelique tells of an agent named Mendenhall who outfitted them poorly but promised to send a boat loaded with additional supplies. So it was they arrived on the island on July 1 with little sustenance to tide them over. Tragically, neither the supplies nor a ride off the island ever arrived.

"Having a bark canoe and a net, for a while we lived on fish, but one day about the end of summer, a storm came and we lost our canoe; and soon our net was broken and good for nothing also. Oh, how we watched and watched and watched, but no bateau (boat) ever came to supply us with food; no vessel ever came to take us away."

At that time, Isle Royale was entirely uninhabited by humans during the winter. Once the cold set in there would be no hope of supplies or rescue until the spring. Angelique had to know that they had been deserted and there would be no getting away for a very long time. Faced with a spartan landscape and being so ill-prepared, starvation became their constant watchman.

"Oh, sir, hunger is an awful thing. It eats you up so inside, and you feel so all gone, as if you must go crazy. Five days before Christmas everything was gone. There was not so much as a single bean. The snow had come down thick and heavy. It was bitter, bitter cold and everything was frozen as hard as stone . . . we drew our belts tighter and tighter; but it was no use; you can't beat hunger; you can't fill up that inward craving that gnaws within you like a wolf."

She tells of Charlie's suffering being much worse. He wasted away until fever set in, rising higher and higher until, she says, he lost his mind. Angelique draws an ugly picture of a scene where her hunger-maddened husband threatens to slaughter a sheep to satisfy his awful hunger, glaring at her with murderous intent as he whet his butcher knife. Never taking her wary eyes from him and tensely waiting, she describes how she finally found her opportunity and valiantly wrested the weapon from his grasp.

Charlie sank further into his wasted body until he faded away. Angelique reports laying his pathetic corpse in their hut, then struggling with the dilemma of either living in the warmth with the dead man, or moving him outdoors. She says that she finally left the cabin and moved to a self-made lodge, carrying her fire with her.

That's when Angelique's real problems began:

" . . . the worst trouble of all. What I had to pray the hardest against was this: Sometimes I was so hungry, so very hungry, and the hunger raged so in my veins that I was tempted, O, how terribly was I tempted to take Charlie and make soup of him. For more than a week I had nothing to eat but bark, and how I prayed that night that the good God would give me something to eat, lest the ever increasing temptation would come over me at last. The next morning when I opened the door I noticed for the first time some rabbit tracks. In a moment I had torn a lock of hair out of my head and was plaiting strands to make a snare for them. That very day I caught one, and so raging hungry was I that I tore off his skin and ate him up raw."

The days and nights of cold and hunger moved slowly for those next five months, with only an occasional rabbit and handfuls of dried vegetation to sustain her. "Oh, how heavily did the time hang upon me," she recounted. "It seemed as if the old moon would never wear out and the new one never come."

In March, she found a wayward, broken canoe on shore. After mending it, she fashioned its sail to be used for a net and thus augmented her meager rations with fish.

One morning in May, salvation arrived, heralded by a gunshot. "Then I heard another gun and started to run down to the landing but my knees gave way and I sank to the ground. Another gun—and I was off to the boat in time to meet the crew when they came ashore. The very first man that landed was Mendenhall and he put up his hand to shake hands with me, which I did. 'Where is Charlie,' said he. I told him he was asleep. He might go up to the hut and see for himself. Then they all ran off together.

"When Mendenhall went into the hut he saw that Charlie was dead. The men took off Charlie's clothes and shoes and saw plain enough that I had not killed him but that he had died of starvation. When I came up Mendenhall began to cry and try to explain things. He said that 'he had sent off a bateau with provisions and didn't see why they didn't get to us.' But the boys told me it was all a lie. I was too glad to get back to my mother to do anything. I thought his own conscience ought to punish him more than I could do."

We are told that Angelique worked in Marquette for some time after leaving the island and that she died at Sault Ste. Marie in 1874. Outside of those meager facts, the rest of her considerable life is lost to the past, despite thorough searches of archives and ledgers. Even though what she is credited with saying seems to be revealing of the most personal thoughts, we feel like maybe we don't really know her at all. At first glance this is a heroine, a woman who suffered terribly and yet prevailed against the worst that nature or man could dish out, against even her most awful desires. How can we not admire her courage, tenacity and moral fortitude?

Then again, what have we but an alleged narration by someone who was the only witness to a tragedy? What else might have happened as those two souls, cut off from the outside world and facing certain death, squared off over the right to stay alive? Could we really blame her if she defended herself from a man driven over the brink of sanity? As far as we know, at the time of her accounting Mendenhall and the prospectors may have been long gone, leaving no one to deny or substantiate her claims.

We don't even know where Charlie's body lies, though popular lore assures us that he is buried on Mott Island, the island that also came to bear his name. And so the story remains yet another mystery in the lengthy and often tragic annals of Lake Superior.

Overhead

BURNING SKY

Somewhere, something incredible is waiting to be known.

—Carl Sagan

Few of us have the occasion or the opportunity to spend much time gazing at the night sky—except, perhaps, a brief glance upward now and then. However, most of us would find it difficult to return indoors on a night when the northern lights are shining, and we've all shared the small thrill of wishing on a shooting star.

These minor instances are what restore our sense of wonder and remind us that the universe is vast and filled with secrets. How much has passed, unwitnessed, overhead either while we slept or while we were too busy to notice?

On January 15, 1985, at 4:30 a.m., something rare and awe-inspiring came blasting to earth from outer space. It passed directly over my home north of Two Harbors in Silver Creek Township, and I was none the wiser. Fortunately, my neighbor Roy Sipper saw it and was able to share the story with me.

My family and I lived three miles west of Lake Superior, and Roy resided a third of a mile south of us along Highway 3. He was outside, on his way to beginning his early morning chores, when he heard what sounded like the snapping and popping of Independence Day fireworks.

Roy looked toward the sky and was surprised to see an object about the size of a small car, no more than a few thousand feet in the air, traveling at great speeds. It zoomed over the top of my house and continued its downward path.

As it roared by him, Roy spotted many different colors—blues and oranges and reds. He soon realized that those colors were actually flames. Large chunks began breaking off the object, and each of them was on fire too.

"Good thing there was snow, or it would've started the woods on fire," said Roy.

Others saw it as well. Bob Hutchison (now deceased) observed the object and wrote about it in the *Lake County Chronicle*. Judging by the object's height and direction of travel, he thought it must have gone down in the lake. If so, Superior has yet to relinquish any pieces of it.

Of course, unlike our other stories of strange objects in the sky, this one has a logical, scientific explanation. What my neighbors saw zipping through the clouds in that early morning was a meteorite. But naming it doesn't make it any less spectacular.

Writing about the incident, I'm reminded of Admiral Robert Peary. While exploring Greenland in the late 1800s he found that some of its indigenous people were in possession of an iron-like metal, which they used for making tools. When Peary inquired where this metal came from, they brought him to a huge rock resting on the surface of the snow pack.

Peary reasoned correctly that it must have been a meteorite. He wanted to take it back to New York and have experts in the field examine it, but due to its massive size and weight, he concluded this would be impossible.

He was also informed that there were smaller pieces of this same object scattered widely over the area. Peary was taken to some of them, but most were too large; eventually, he found one that he could manage and he brought it back with him to New York.

Astronomers from the Museum of Natural History confirmed that it was indeed a meteorite. When the scientists learned that it was only a small piece of a far larger object, they were intrigued. They implored Peary to retrieve the rest of the meteorite. Through some very dogged effort and novel feats of engineering, the next year Peary retrieved the 32-ton chunk he had originally encountered and managed to load it on a ship.

Back in New York, he still needed to unload the giant space rock and move it through the streets to the museum. City officials were afraid it might crash through the streets and into the subway tunnels beneath. Apparently this did not happen and the massive extraterrestrial stone resides in the museum to this day.

As for our meteorite, whatever became of it is officially unknown, but more likely than not, Hutchison is correct: It rests in the cold, deep waters of Lake Superior. Or perhaps it simply passed us by on its way to the Canadian tundra. Either way—and whether or not it is ever is found—we will still never learn from where it came.

BALL LIGHTNING?

Don't bog me down with talk of protons and ions. This is mystical stuff.

—Sam Cook, Quiet Magic

A man whom we will only call "Don" ran a small sawmill back in the 1970s and '80s. He was a familiar face and a respected member of the Two Harbors area. Before he passed away, he shared with me a bizarre encounter from his younger days.

One night when Don had trouble sleeping, he got up to fetch a glass of water. As he returned to his bedroom, he noticed a softball-sized object glowing brightly upon the sill outside his window.

Not one to believe in such "nonsense" as the paranormal, Don was certain that his eyes were playing tricks on him. But suddenly, the globe rolled off the sill and fell into his yard. Curiosity got the better of him, so Don scurried to his window to take a look. He watched in disbelief as the glowing object bounced across his yard and into the woods. Dumbfounded, Don returned to bed. Needless to say, the strange encounter did not aid him in getting to sleep that night.

Years later, as Don and I spoke of the event, it was clear that he was still puzzled by it. The two of us discussed the possibility that it may have been what is known as "ball lightning." I've read that such a phenomenon does—on occasion—occur, and it can act in peculiar ways. In fact, to this day, the scientific community does not fully understand it.

Reports of ball lightning date back hundreds of years. In many incidents, it is said to float or hover in midair. Through the years, it has often been described as basketball sized (though sometimes smaller) and teardrop or spherical in shape. Many reports of ball lightning have been associated with thunderstorms, but not all. Some stem from clear days, further deepening the mystery.

Ball lightning is also offered as one explanation for the strange fireballs that sometimes appeared off the wingtips of Allied airplanes during nighttime missions in World War II. At the time, pilots thought the balls of light emanated from enemy fighters and referred to them as "foo fighters." The lights were reported in both the European and Pacific theatres. After the war, military experts became convinced the odd lights were not from any form of Axis aircraft.

Of course, ball lightning is just one possible explanation for what Don saw that night. What else it could have been is anyone's guess. Glowing balls of light represent a small but substantial portion of the literature on the paranormal. Whatever it was Don saw on that night so long ago seemed to make a lasting impression on him. I invite you to decide for yourself what you think it might have been.

CURIOUSER AND CURIOUSER

It was the darnedest thing I've ever seen. It was big, it was very bright, it changed colors and it was about the size of the moon . . . one thing's for sure, I'll never make fun of people who say they've seen unidentified objects in the sky. If I become President, I'll make every piece of information this country has about UFO sightings available to the public and the scientists.

—Jimmy Carter, on the campaign trail in 1976

At first glance 1992 may appear to be an inconspicuous year, but the superstitious among us will notice that the sum of its digits (1 + 9 + 9 + 2) equals twenty-one, a mystical number of luck and good fortune. It's likely you're somewhat familiar with this lucky number. For instance, have you ever tried to spin triple sevens on your favorite slot machine?

Mystical or not, 1992 was certainly unusual in that Lake Superior froze completely over that year, something it rarely does. The following account, which took place at a home along Lake Superior's shores in Duluth, provides further evidence of the abnormal. It began when a man saw—through his living room window—several lights sitting atop the ice, perhaps a mile from the harbor.

Intrigued, he sat down to observe, wondering if he might see something unusual. After a few moments, he witnessed an occurrence more than merely odd. It was downright paranormal. One by one, the lights rose into the air and streaked away in a flash. The man was so dumbfounded that he nearly fell out of his chair.

I was fortunate enough to speak with the man just a few days later. He was absolutely moved by what he had seen, and it had most certainly changed his life. To this day, he believes that he now has proof, beyond a shadow of a doubt, that we are not alone in the universe. After all, he has seen it with his own eyes.

Another strange sighting reported to me in 1992 took place

on a drive between Duluth and Two Harbors. A local resort owner pulled to the side of the road late one evening to answer nature's call. He was on old Highway 61 at the time, just northeast of the old pumping station.

As he stood on the side of the road, taking care of business, his attention was drawn toward two mysterious sets of lights in the nearby sky. They were moving in tandem along the lakeshore just a few hundred feet in the air. He concluded that two small planes were out for an evening flight and silently wondered if their passengers could see him. Yet something other than the fear of embarrassment troubled him. It was only a moment before he realized what it was: The "planes" weren't making any noise—not a sound.

He further noticed that the objects in the sky each cast two beams of light downward, similar to floodlights. The strange aircraft continued their silent journey northward along the shoreline. They passed right next to the driver and his still-running car, and they continued along the lake edge scanning the beach. After a few moments, they disappeared beyond the horizon.

The man may or may not have seen the supernatural, but to this day he refuses to believe it. He maintains the theory that he must have seen top-secret, cutting-edge, experimental military aircraft.

You may also have seen the unexplainable in your life. If so, you no doubt remember it quite well. However, it is probably not a topic you would care to discuss with just anyone—perhaps a family member or close friend.

Indeed, when the subject of strange lights in the sky is raised, most of us are comfortable only to offer tongue-in-cheek jokes about little green men from Mars. Tales of alien abductions and unspeakable probing at the hands of glassy-eyed kidnappers are easily laughed off as the wild delusions of people in need of medication.

But when the crowd thins, the sun sets—and perhaps a few cocktails have lowered our guard—some of us will admit that we too have seen strange things in the night sky—things that have come to be known as Unidentified Flying Objects.

THE DEPUTY'S REPORT

The truth is out there . . .

—*Chris Carter, creator of* The X-Files

Deputy Fred DuFresne served with the Lake County Sheriff's Department for 27 years. He is a steady, cautious man with a practical nature. Perhaps that's why the story he tells is such a shock. Yet he is so certain that an experience which occurred early in his career—on a cold, winter night in 1973—was real, he is willing, even eager, to discuss it without a hint of doubt or embarrassment.

On that fateful night, DuFresne was assigned to road patrol. He was driving around the area, making sure that the citizens of Lake County were safely tucked away. Those late-night shifts were typically uneventful, so it was common for even the most diligent of county employees to occasionally gaze toward the stars, simply taking in the beautiful sights of the heavens. Yet on this particular evening, DuFresne couldn't have guessed the surprise that Minnesota's northern sky had in store for him. For the deputy, this was to be a shift like no other.

Driving down a lonesome road just two miles from the western edge of Two Harbors, DuFresne glanced upward and noticed an odd sight. Just above him, directly over the road, a large object hovered. It was dark, so DuFresne wanted a better look. He brought his cruiser to a stop and climbed outside. He looked up and was immediately struck by the immense size of the aircraft silently hanging over him, just a few hundred feet off the ground. As DuFresne described it, "The craft was oblong and the size of an airliner."

With shaking hands he called his dispatcher, asking him to contact the Duluth Air Force Base to see if anything was showing up on radar. The dispatcher complied and promised to get back to the deputy.

As he waited, DuFresne began to notice "lights of every color—red, blue and green," emanating from the unidentified object in the sky. He watched in wonder for two minutes, awestruck by the object's beauty and sheer size.

When the dispatcher radioed back, he told DuFresne that the air base reported no blips on its screens at that location. One can only imagine that DuFresne, alone and clearly in the presence of the paranormal, must have been terrified.

Deputy DuFresne cannot say for certain what happened next. In fact, he found the incident's ending quite difficult to put into words. He doesn't recall with any sense of clarity how the aircraft left. More accurately, he simply came to realization that it was no longer there. He believes that it must have ascended directly upward at a very rapid speed.

Days later, a local fisherman reported a similar incident. He claimed to have seen an object of nearly identical description hovering above a nearby lake.

Now retired for eleven years, Fred DuFresne still has no hesitation about going on record with his story. "I know what I saw, and it was real," says the former deputy. Despite the fact that certain individuals tried time and again to persuade him that he only saw a reflection from the ice and snow, DuFresne remains certain of his encounter.

Hearing the conviction in his voice and the emotion in his retelling, this author has no doubt that—at the very least—he believes his own story. Whether or not you choose to do the same is completely up to you.

A LIFE-CHANGING INTERVIEW

*The most beautiful thing we can experience is the
mysterious. It is the source of all true art and all science.
He to whom this emotion is a stranger, who can no longer
pause to wonder and stand rapt in awe, is as good as dead:
his eyes are closed.*

—Albert Einstein

More than one person has had their life changed by a visit
from extraterrestrials. The late Robert "Bob" Pratt was
one of them. Though he never saw a UFO, this straight-
forward journalist discovered a new purpose in life thanks to a
paranormal investigation that included a series of interviews—
the most unforgettable with an old bachelor living near Knife
River, Minnesota. This man in particular, and the story that he
related, may have changed Bob Pratt forever.

In the fall of 1974, Adolph Birkland was enjoying his
retirement—away from the Lake Superior ore docks. He
was a small man, further reduced in stature by the process of
aging. He lived alone in a small house at the end of a
dirt road.

Birkland didn't get many visitors out that way, even fewer
in the middle of the night, which is why he was so surprised
late one evening to see a strange, intense light shining into
his home.

His first thought was that a car must be driving up the road
with its "brights" on, but Birkland wondered who in the
world that might be. The entire house seemed to be lit up,
"as bright as day." Birkland crawled out of bed to find out
who his unexpected visitor was, then saw the source of the
lights through the kitchen window—coming from behind the
house, not in front of it.

As Birkland described it, "I saw this thing just come sailing in
slowly from the woods, cross the river and just come floating
across my garden."

The object silently inched along, all the while glowing "something terrible." Considering the amount of light it was emanating, the object was quite small: about six feet long and less than a foot thick. The bright, white lights shining into the house were mounted on the top and bottom of the object. On the side were six or seven smaller, red, teardrop-shaped reflectors.

"Talk about light," said Birkland. "You could see just as plain all the way to the end of the garden."

The object continued hovering at a snail's pace. When it passed behind Birkland's woodshed, everything suddenly went black. The object seemed to disappear, and that was the last he ever saw of it.

According to Pratt, Birkland talked quietly without emotion or expression. After he finished his story, he stared at the floor for a minute or two then quietly added, "It was really nice to see, though. It was pretty—prettiest thing I've ever seen in my life."

By the end of the investigative series, the course of Mr. Pratt's life was redirected. The reporter was so moved by the statements he'd heard that he spent the remainder of his career—and ensuing retirement years—investigating, studying and writing about the intriguing phenomenon of UFO sightings.

As anyone who's ever looked into this subject knows, reports of strange lights in the sky and kindred occurrences happen the world over. Some experts believe that certain areas of the planet attract the paranormal. It is the opinion of these authors that the region in and around the Great Lakes—and Lake Superior in particular—is one of these hotspots for the strange.

Whatever it is that generate these odd lights, whatever these vehicles are (with their apparent disregard for the laws of physics), the question must be asked: What does it mean for us? The thing to remember is, if they were dangerous or meant to control us through superior technology, we would surely have come to harm long ago.

Perhaps, as some radical physicists suggest, our universe, and the dimension it occupies, is only one of many. If there are indeed parallel universes, strange lights and other supernatural phenomena may be accounted for by the movements of incarnations from one dimension to the next. Possibly, whatever strange beings exist today have always shared the Earth with us and call the planet home as well.

Whether you're a believer or a skeptic, you must confess that the realm of the unknown adds a fascinating dimension to the world. And, at the very least, the exploration of the curious provides an endless source of wonder and entertainment.

OUT OF A CLEAR BLUE SKY

*Any sufficiently advanced technology is indistinguishable
from magic.*

—Arthur C. Clarke, Profiles of the Future, 1961

Sometimes the paranormal seeks out those of us who are
fascinated with it. Such is the case for a former North Shore
resident who has since relocated to the Twin Cities. This
man, who chose to remain nameless, had more than a casual
interest in the supernatural, but one brief encounter turned
his leisurely ponderings into instant, unquestionable truth.

Unlike most UFO sightings, his story takes place in broad
daylight—more specifically at approximately 11 a.m. on
February 28, 1990. It was a sunny, almost cloudless day.
The man was driving a close friend, his mother and his
grandfather south along old Highway 61, on their way to the
airport in Minneapolis.

The scenery along that stretch of road may be picturesque,
but it was a drive all too familiar to the car's occupants.
It's understandable why everyone except the driver was
falling under its spell, nodding off to sleep. It seemed like an
ordinary trip, but it turned out to be anything but.

In the distance to the right, the driver suddenly spotted a
silver-white object, flying perhaps a thousand feet above the
ground. Moving from west to east, the object was no more
than a few hundred yards away.

"Look at that," he shouted, but it was moving too quickly.
By the time the words escaped his mouth, it was nearly
past them.

Sleepy eyes jolted open, as the silvery aircraft intersected
the car's path. Too slowly for two of the passengers, the
world came into focus. Fortunately, the man's mother had
been slightly more awake than the other two. She turned
around and looked out the back window, catching sight of
the strange object.

The man slowed his car almost to a stop, straining hard to look back over his left shoulder. He watched the flying object tip downward in the general direction of Lake Superior. It was at that moment when he got his best look at the ship, which he later described as disc-shaped, about thirty feet in circumference, thicker in the middle but tapering toward its edges. As it moved, it seemed to wobble or oscillate in some strange way.

The man lost sight of the object in the horizon, and the car became abuzz as the passengers compared notes. Compelled to continue driving in order to make their flight, they discussed the strange event. The man's mother and he agreed on the object's general size, appearance and that it seemed to be headed toward the surface of the lake.

When hearing a report such as this, one always questions the source. However, the man in this story is known to the authors. He is educated, intelligent and, as a reporter, has a keen eye for detail. Furthermore, his honesty and reliability are unquestioned. With that said, I believe that almost any of us would be able to recognize a bird, plane, helicopter or kite—most certainly from that distance on a bright, clear day.

This reporter had nothing to gain and everything to lose by sharing such a tale (which, in part, is why he chose to remain anonymous). Yet, to this day, he maintains the validity of his sighting.

Certainly a large portion of the unexplained has a reasonable, scientific explanation. People make mistakes and are perfectly capable of fabricating stories out of thin air for the amusement of themselves or for others. But I cannot believe that every report, every instance, is a mistake or a lie. Some of these events must be real and therefore merit closer examination. The mystery is what makes these stories interesting, and what good would a mystery be if we already knew the answer?

LOST AIRMEN

O lost, and by the wind grieved ghost, come back again.

—*Thomas Wolf,* Look Homeward Angel

Over the years, some tales of the strange take on lives of their own. Such is the case with the fascinating story of an ill-fated U.S. Air Force F-89 Scorpion fighter jet, which vanished from radar while investigating an unidentified flying object over Lake Superior more than fifty years ago.

Although the aircraft's mysterious demise has been the source of speculation and controversy since the plane's disappearance over the great inland sea, recent assertions by a Michigan-based dive company have catapulted the unlucky F-89 and its two-man crew back into the spotlight. The company claims to have found the lost Scorpion—as well as the mystery object with which it collided. Backing those claims are controversial sonar images the company says depict the stricken jet and a UFO lying near each other in the murky depths of Lake Superior.

Let's start at the beginning: On the evening of November 23, 1953, at approximately 6 p.m., Lt. Felix Moncla and Lt. Robert Wilson were scrambled in their F-89 Scorpion interceptor jet from Kinross Air Force Base near Sault Ste Marie, Michigan. Their mission was to investigate an Identify Friend or Foe (IFF) flying at high speeds over Lake Superior. Whether or not the unidentified object was ever technically in U.S. territory is unclear. However, it was obviously considered a serious enough threat that it warranted a closer look.

During his flight, Lt. Moncla reported moderately unstable weather conditions with snow showers and possible icing problems. At one point, he requested permission to return to the base. The pilot was advised to proceed from that point onward at his own discretion. Moncla also encountered problems maintaining radio contact with his base, but the Kinross operators did manage to keep constant radar contact with him.

Forty minutes into his flight, Moncla was advised that the IFF was maintaining a steady course at a speed of five hundred miles per hour and would be nearing his port wing directly. The lieutenant requested permission to descend from his elevation of thirty thousand feet down to seven thousand in order to clear the cloud canopy, presumably in an attempt to make visual contact. Permission was granted, and the pilot descended. Neither Lt. Moncla nor Lt. Wilson were ever heard from again.

Radar operators monitoring the situation, both at Kinross and elsewhere, saw the two blips near each other, then apparently merge for a few seconds. Some reports say that the IFF continued along its path while the F-89 suddenly disappeared roughly 70 miles northeast of Michigan's Keweenaw Peninsula. However, official reports—while unclear—seem to indicate that both blips disappeared a few seconds after converging. In truth, several accounts of the incident exist, and it is certain that either no one really knows or no one is saying exactly what happened.

Within minutes of Moncla and Wilson's disappearance, two additional F-89 interceptors—piloted by Lt. William Mingenbach and Second Lt. Howard Nordeck—were launched in an attempt to make visual, radio or radar contact with the missing jet. Upon arriving at the Scorpion's last known whereabouts, Lt. Mingenbach reported dense cloud cover and a low ceiling no higher than three thousand feet. He indicated concern for the safety of his ship and ascended to an altitude of twenty thousand feet, where he circled, continuing his attempts to make radio or radar contact. After a time, he reported that no such response was forthcoming, and he returned to base.

Weather records and Moncla's own transmissions suggest that flying conditions were somewhat problematic on that fateful evening. However, for reasons unknown, the Air Force did not release its official report of the accident until December 27—more than a month later. The report seemed to rule out any questions of Lt. Moncla's health and any potential mechanical problems as causes of the disappearance. In fact, Moncla and his Scorpion had made an uneventful routine flight earlier that same day.

Coincidentally, Moncla and Wilson were not the day's first casualties. Earlier, another F-89 from the duo's own fighter group had crashed in a freak accident, resulting in the deaths of two men whom Moncla and Wilson knew well. The loss likely weighed heavily on their hearts and minds. Little did they know that it foreshadowed their own fates.

Like so many aircraft lost in the Bermuda Triangle, the F-89 Scorpion seemed to vanish forever. For more than fifty years its mystery remained intact, until it was almost forgotten. But this tragic tale doesn't end there.

On September 22, 2006, well-known author of the paranormal Linda Moulton Howe (www.earthfiles.com) was a guest on the popular, late-night, radio talk show Coast to Coast AM. During the broadcast, the Emmy Award-winning documentary producer announced that she was in contact with one Adam Jimenez, the owner of an underwater dive company who had located wreckage from the ill-fated F-89 Scorpion.

As the broadcast continued, Howe contacted Jimenez via telephone, and he related to the national audience that he and his crew from the Great Lakes Dive Company had in fact, while on an unrelated 2005 expedition, accidentally stumbled upon what appeared to be the remains of a jet aircraft. Furthermore, his expedition had also discovered an additional object of unknown origin.

Needless to say, Jimenez and his crew were shocked by their unexpected discovery. They were aware of the missing aircraft and logically concluded that they had found the remains of the fifty-year-old Scorpion. Uncertain what to do about the unidentified object sunken with the jet, they sat on their information for nearly a year before revealing it to Howe, high priestess of the strange.

In the months following the September 22 interview, Jimenez posted physical evidence of his discovery—in the form of enhanced sonar images—online. At this writing, a simple Internet search produced numerous references to the Great Lakes Dive Company, quotes from Jimenez and images purportedly from the F-89 crash site. Oddly though, the company's own website has disappeared—and accusations of a hoax are circulating as well.

This latest development doesn't answer many questions. In fact, it only adds to the confusion surrounding the missing Scorpion. What brought this unfortunate craft and crew to the freezing depths of Lake Superior? All that we have to go on are a few limited and frequently conflicting facts.

The official conclusion, made by accident investigator Capt. David Collins (and corroborated by Col. James Cornett, Chief Investigator of Safety Engineering Division), was that our IFF was actually a Canadian RCAF Dakota C-47 jet fighter flying from Winnipeg, Manitoba, to Sudbury, Ontario. Yet Collins' conclusion offers no explanation as to why the C-47 did not respond to Moncla's repeated attempts to make radio contact. It is possible, of course, that the radio problems Moncla reported shortly before the Scorpion disappeared might have prevented the C-47 from making contact.

The Canadian pilot, according to his brief account, observed nothing unusual on the night of November 23, 1953. He maintained his course at an elevation of approximately seven thousand feet, without mishap, and he arrived at Sudbury on schedule. Many years later, the same pilot maintained in a telephone interview with a private investigator that he was never in United States airspace and could not possibly have been off course, due to the sophisticated nature of his jet's navigational system.

Another explanation, offered by the U.S. Air Force years after their initial reports were debunked, suggests that the unidentified radar image was a commercial DC-3 airplane—one that had never filed a flight plan with American officials. Or if they had filed a flight plan, it never reached the desks of radar operators at Kinross.

There is little doubt that other aircraft were in the vicinity of the F-89 on the night of its disappearance. But again, why would they have maintained radio silence? Or, if recognized, why would they have been perceived as a threat? The only logical conclusion is that something else must have been present on air force radar screens that night—something that disappeared just as mysteriously as it had first appeared.

Today, we have two mysteries before us: First, and most perplexing, what happened to that F-89 Scorpion on the night of November 23, 1953? Secondly, what has become of our friend Mr. Jimenez? Without him, it's impossible to determine what the unidentified object is in the Great Lakes Dive Company images, and perhaps more importantly, where it is located on the vast floor of Lake Superior.

If in fact Mr. Jimenez and his company have found our lost fighter and its crew, wouldn't it be a simple matter to give those coordinates to Air Force officials, who could then possibly retrieve the remains of the crew or at the very least verify their location, and relieve the lingering doubts that must still remain in the hearts and minds of any living relatives.

Apparently though, nothing like this has occurred. And Mr. Jimenez has not been heard from since. Perhaps he has been instructed to remain silent due to complications arising from the fact that the fighter jet lies well within Canadian waters—not to speak further about it until the red tape of international politics is sorted out. Or possibly, his silence stems from hopes for personal gain. Then again, the whole "discovery" could be nothing more than a cruel hoax.

It would seem that once a thing has entered the realm of the bizarre, once it has crossed from this world into another, the forces that drew it away exert a power that would keep it secret forever. Everyone has heard the story of the bygone planes and aviators of Flight 19, lost more than half a century ago off the coast of Florida. All five planes and their crews, flying in good weather on a routine mission over what has been called the Bermuda Triangle, were lost from radar and radio contact and never seen again. No wreckage was found, not a life raft, not an oil slick.

Hopefully, this isn't the case with the F-89. We can only hope that the Great Lakes Dive Company did in fact locate its wreckage, and one day soon, the Air Force may bring the remains of Lt. Moncla and Wilson home.

Perhaps we may resolve some of these long-standing questions, but the exact circumstances surrounding the end of this craft and her crew will likely never be completely known. Sadly, the fact remains that on an ordinary winter night in November of 1953, Lt. Felix Moncla and Lt. Robert Wilson boarded an airship in service to their country and its citizens, went forth to meet a mystery and flew off into eternity.

ABOUT THE AUTHORS

Bill Mayo is a former Duluth resident and has lived in Two Harbors, Minnesota, for the last twenty-three years. Long a part of the poetry scene of the North Shore and a former Artist-in-Residence for Isle Royale National Park, he has published work in *National Geographic Traveler, Poets Who Haven't Moved to St. Paul* and *Zenith City Arts*. He also holds an AAS Degree in Human Services and is an enrolled member of the Leech Lake Pillager Band. His love of the North Shore came early while driving along old Highway 61 with his parents as a boy. Whether in a canoe, diving or walking the beach, the eternal mystery of the lake is always awe-inspiring for him.

A Minnesota native and longtime visitor to the North Shore, Kate Barthel now resides within view of Lake Superior. Frequent trips "Up North" finally gave over to permanent residence, and Kate has drawn on her previous perspective as a visitor to the area in the compilation of these narratives. She spent most of her career in the role of counselor, is a licensed therapist and addictions counselor with an MA in counseling psychology.